A HOSPITAL ST

JA

JUN

This paperback edition published in 1984.

Published simultaneously in Canada by John
Wiley & Sons Canada, Limited, Rexdale, Ontario.

ISBN: 0-8027-7222-6

Library of Congress Catalog Card Number: 73-15269

Printed in the United States of America.

10 9 8 7 6 5 4 3 2

A HOSPITAL STORY

An Open Family Book For Parents And Children Together

by Sara Bonnett Stein

in cooperation with
Gilbert W. Kliman, M.D.
Director

Doris Ronald
Educational Director,
The Cornerstone Nursery-Kindergarten

Ann S. Kliman
Director,
Situational Crisis Service

Phyllis Schwartz
Community Coordinator

The Center for Preventive
Psychiatry
White Plains, New York

photography by Doris Pinney
graphic design, Michel Goldberg

Walker and Company
New York, New York
Created by Media Projects Incorporated

A Note About This Book

When your child was a baby, you took him to the doctor to have him immunized for childhood illnesses. The injections hurt a little, but you knew they would prepare his body to cope with far more serious threats in the future. Yet there are other threats as painful and destructive to a child's growth as physical illness: Separation from his parents, a death in the family, a new baby, fears and fantasies of his own imagining that hurt as much as pain itself. These Open Family Books are to help adults prepare children for common hurts of childhood.

Caring adults try to protect their child from difficult events. But still that child has ears that overhear, eyes that read the faces of adults around him. If people are sad, he knows it. If people are worried, he knows it. If people are angry, he knows that too.

What he doesn't know—if no one tells him—is the whole story. In his attempts to make sense of what is going on around him, he fills in the fragments he has noticed with fantasied explanations of his own which, because he is a child, are often more frightening than the truth.

We protect children because we know them to be different, more easily damaged than ourselves. But the difference we sense is not widely understood. Children are more easily damaged because they cannot make distinctions yet between what is real and what is unreal, what is magic and what is logic. The tiger under a child's bed at night is as real to him as the tiger in the zoo. When he wishes a bad thing, he believes his wish can make the bad thing happen. His fearful imagining about what is going on grips him because he has no way to test the truth of it.

It is the job of parents to support and explain reality, to guide a child toward the truth even if it is painful. The dose may be small, just as a dose of vaccine is adjusted to the smallness of a baby; but even if it is a little at a time, it is only straightforwardness that gives children the internal strength to deal with things not as they imagine them to be, but as they are.

To do that, parents need to understand what sorts of fears, fantasies, misunderstandings are common to early childhood—what they might expect at three years old, or at five, or seven. They need simpler ways to explain the way complicated things are. The adult text of each of these books, in the left hand column, explains extraordinary ways that ordinary children between three and eight years old attempt to make sense of difficult events in their lives. It puts in words uncomplicated ways to say things. It is probably best to read the adult text several times before you read the book to your child, so you will get a comfortable feel for the ideas and so you won't be distracted as you talk together. If your child can read, he may one day be curious to read the adult text. That's all right. What's written there is the same as what you are talking about together. The pictures and the words in large print are to start the talking between you and your child. The stories are intense enough to arouse curiosity and feeling. But they are reasonable, forthright and gentle, so a child can deal with the material at whatever level he is ready for.

The themes in these Open Family Books are common to children's play. That is no accident. Play, joyous but also serious, is the way a child enacts himself a little bit at a time, to get used to events, thoughts and feelings he is confused about. Helping a child keep clear on the difference between what is real and what is fantasy will not restrict a child's creativity in play. It will let him use fantasy more freely because it is less frightening.

In some ways, these books won't work. No matter how a parent explains things, a child will misunderstand some part of the explanation, sometimes right away, sometimes in retrospect, weeks or even months later. Parents really can't help this fact of psychological life. Nothing in human growing works all at once, completely or forever. But parents can keep the channels of communication open so that gradually their growing child can bring his version of the way things are closer to the reality. Each time you read an Open Family Book and talk about it together, your child will take in what at that moment is most useful to him. Another day, another month, years later, other aspects of the book will be useful to him in quite different ways. The book will not have changed; what he needs, what he notices, how he uses it will change.

But that is what these books are for: To open between adult and child the potential for growth that exists in human beings of all ages.

Sometimes doctors aren't too ready to explain things. And sometimes people aren't too sure about asking them. But if a doctor has just advised an operation, you are probably thinking things that worry you, and your child is probably thinking things that worry him. You will have to dare to ask. Your doctor will probably be patient enough to answer.

The questions we ask often sound funny, dumb, mixed up, exaggerated, because no one ever told us much about what we're like inside —where things are and how they work, and what will happen if something's done to them. We were confused when we were children, and we can still be confused now. But we can say to a doctor, "You know, I used to think tonsils were cut off with scissors (or a hernia meant something was torn, or pneumonia is a sickness you always die of), and no one ever really explained it to me." Then he will see how long these childhood confusions last and help you and your child get to know your bodies better.

Jill is at the doctor's. "Her tonsils are making her sick," says Dr. James. "I'm sorry, but they have to come out."

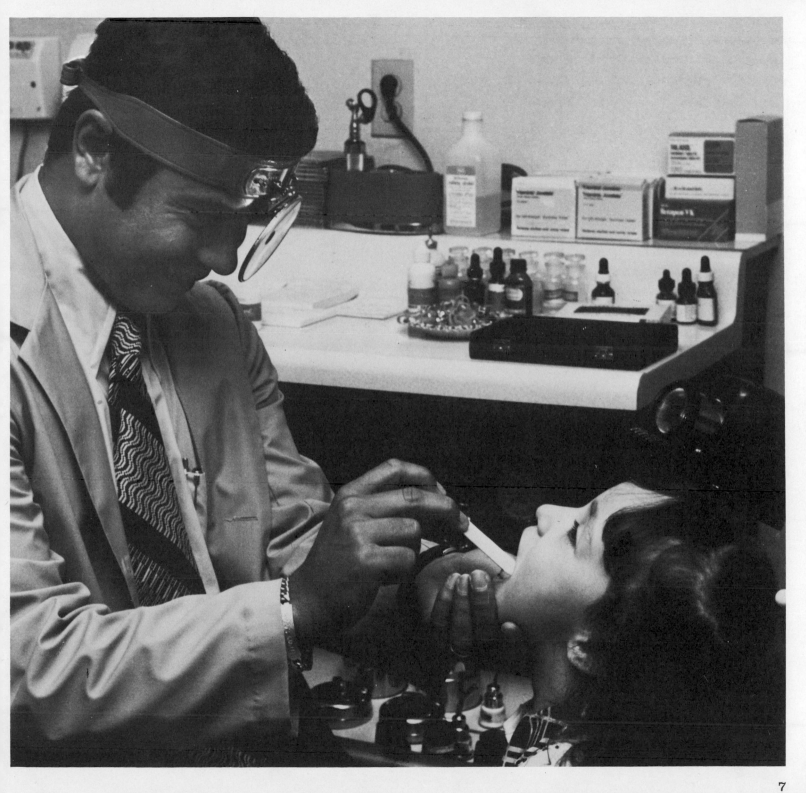

Who could like someone poking around in his body, and who could like someone taking a piece of it away? People don't like intrusions they can't control. That is basic.

When a child's very own body must be intruded into, we might as well agree it is unpleasant and hard for a child to go through. We might even say that it is quite all right to be mad at the nurse who jabs a hole into his finger. It is quite all right to be mad at the doctor who is too interested in what's up his nose or in his belly. It is quite all right to be angry, if that is how he feels.

Jill doesn't want her tonsils out. She doesn't want anyone to do anything to her.

There is an odd way of feeling that all we humans share. It is called ambivalence. It means we can like someone and not like him at the same time. It means we can trust a doctor to make us well and be certain he will do something terrible. It means we ourselves sometimes say, "I'm sorry," even though we feel quite pleased with the hurting things we are doing.

When Jill plays with Dodie, she is caring for her and hurting her, being good to her and punishing her. She is doing to Dodie what she thinks is being done to her. Every time Jill plays this doctor game, she lets herself feel a little scared. And every time she plays it, she feels stronger about her fears, gets more used to having to be, for a while, like her Dodie.

Dodie is sick too. She has to have lots and lots of shots. "Sorry, we have to cut you," says Jill. She puts Band-aids on Dodie.

For everything that could be wrong with a child, he can probably think of it in mistaken ways that are even worse.

Some of the mistakes children make are because they misunderstand what they see: They see in the back of their mouth the uvula that moves when they talk, and so they may think that is their tonsils and when it is gone they will have no voice.

Some of the mistakes are because they misunderstand what they hear: Germs are "catching," so maybe they really catch you. They are "bugs," so they bite you inside. If tonsils are described as "little balls," a child may think they are the same as testicles. If an appendix is described as "a little finger," a child may think that is too valuable a part of his body to give up.

Some of the mistakes are because of what they know about objects: When the handle of a cup is broken, it is broken off; so maybe that's what a broken leg is like. When a bucket has a hole in it, all the water comes out; so they often think if the doctor makes a hole in your skin, all the blood will come out. When a machine loses a part, it doesn't work at all; so they wonder how they can work if a part of them is missing.

Asking a child to explain things to you, helping him to draw a picture, are ways to find out what he is mixed up about. Then it is your turn to explain, to show him the way it really is. A child may still be afraid, but he is less scared if he knows the adults he trusts are willing to explain.

Jill and her mommy are drawing a picture because it is hard to understand about operations. They talk about where her tonsils are and what happens when they are taken out.

It is easy to understand why grownups promise good things to children and hide the bad. They are sorry, really, to hurt a child. But it is lonely for a child to worry all by himself. And anyhow, he can see what your face is saying as easily as you can see into his.

If you feel awful that he will have to be without you some of the time, say so. If he wonders how someone can be cut and still be okay, or whether his sickness is very serious, talk about it together.

Go easy on those good promises. "It won't hurt" is not a promise, but a lie. You will not be there "whenever he needs you," because you could be grabbing a cup of coffee in the cafeteria or making a call from the pay phone down the hall or going to the bathroom. There may be a wonderful playroom, but he may not be in the mood for it right then. There may be all the ice cream he can eat, but he may feel too sick to eat it. And you might give him the biggest teddy bear in the whole world, when all he wants is to get out of that place, back to his mommy and daddy—home safe!

Jill is worried about going to the hospital. She isn't sure what it will be like. But now it is time to pack her suitcase and to go.

You can do your best to prepare your child, and still the hospital will be strange and shocking. It smells like nothing he has smelled before. He has not seen what really sick people look like. There may be wheelchairs, stretchers, casts and crutches. It will seem a place to get lost in—halls, rooms, stairways, elevators, doors—that do not tell you where you are, or how to find the way out. The pictures in this book purposely show details to talk about. A doctor or nurse can help you explain what's what. Sometimes a hospital will have its own brochure with photographs, and that will help too.

Some schools take children on a field trip to the local hospital. That is very helpful because they are all together, healthy, unharmed, but getting used to hospitals all the same.

Jill's mother has borrowed a Polaroid camera to take with her to the hospital. They will take pictures of places and people Jill chooses. Then when she is home again, the pictures will let her check out her memory of what the hospital was like and what really happened there.

This is the hospital. It looks strange. It smells funny.

17

All through the first years of child-hood, boys and girls are working hard to hold onto their own reins in one way and another—to keep their temper, to control their bladder, to handle their fears, and to whisper, to skip, to tie, to button, to draw a straight line. That is what we expect of them. That is how we and they have proof of their growing.

Now, in the hospital, a child will not be able to control much at all. His mother and father, who have been his controls before he had any, who have helped him slowly to take over on his own, will not have much say either. It is a double danger: No chance to run things himself. No parents to take over for him.

Though they have no rule about it, this hospital has offered Jill a ride in a wheelchair. Jill lets Dodie try that. She pushes the elevator button all by herself. Small controls, but they help.

Jill gets a bracelet on her wrist with her name on it. Dodie tries a wheelchair. They go upstairs in the elevator.

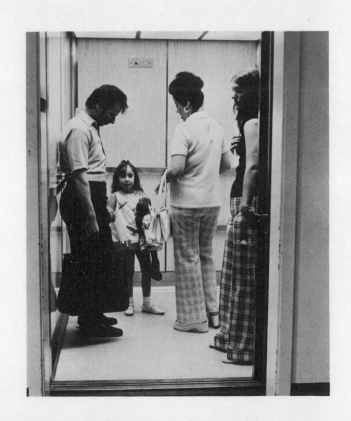

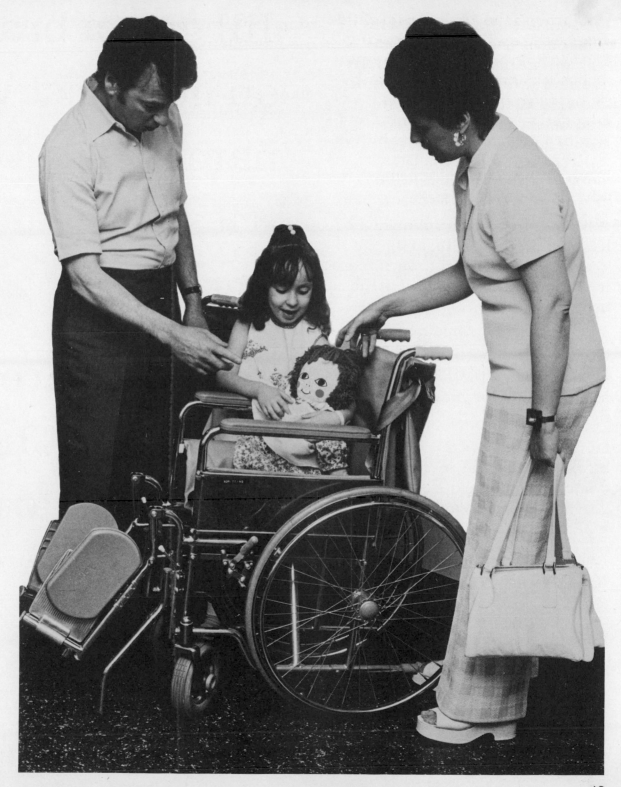

Find out ahead of time what the rules and procedures are. That way, no one has to argue with anyone; and a child can draw comfort knowing all the grownups are together, strong like a wall is strong, just when he needs it.

Find out the details of routine admission procedure.

Get a picture or description of the hospital room—whether it is shared with other children, if there is a telephone or TV set, what the beds are like.

Ask what your child can wear, whether he can bring toys or books with him, what the visiting hours are, and whether you can stay overnight.

Get a rundown of a typical child's day in the hospital, including what doctors and nurses visit him, when temperatures are taken, what meals are like.

Ask about routine and special tests your child will have—and whether they hurt, are uncomfortable, take a long time, use unfamiliar equipment.

See if your doctor can tell you ahead of time as much as he can about any medicines, shots, special diets, casts, traction apparatus, stitches, dressings, medical procedures or physical restric-

tions your child will need so they can be explained too.

And ask about when he's back at home—what will his convalescence really be like?

These are nurses. They wear special clothes. They will help Jill's parents take care of her in the hospital.

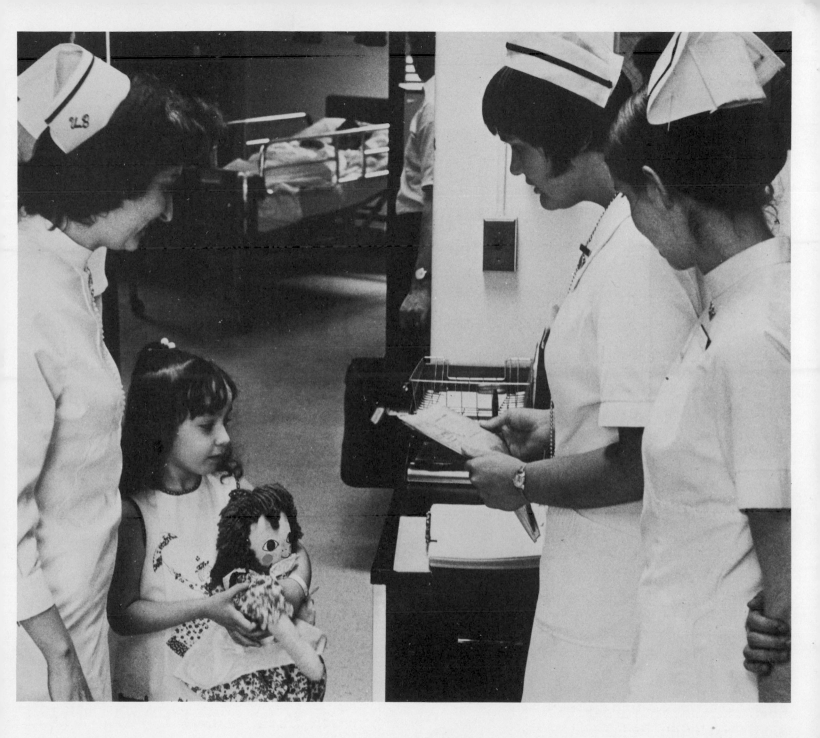

In a hospital what is happening all around can be unnerving. Other children crying. A child with his leg in traction. A child with bandages over his eyes. A child with burns. A child with something very wrong with an arm, an ear. Or a child trying to walk for the first time after an appendectomy.

There is no need to recite possibilities before they occur, but there is need to take on what happens as it comes. When you see that stiff, scared glance on your child's face or when he gets wild or silly so you know he's upset, open up a little so he can too. Something like, "Gee, it really seems to hurt him to walk." Or, "It always bothers me to see bandages on someone's face." Trust yourself to guess at what's worrying him, and help by bringing it out in the open, sharing the worry together. Perhaps a nurse will help you with the explanations. "He does have his eye under the bandage, but it is being fixed." "It hurts to walk just after that operation, but he will walk fine in a few days." "That isn't a sickness you can catch, it's a burn on his arm." "She was born with that kind of ear. The doctor can make it look better."

Jill sees things that bother her. Mommy and Daddy explain how doctors fix people, even when they are very sick.

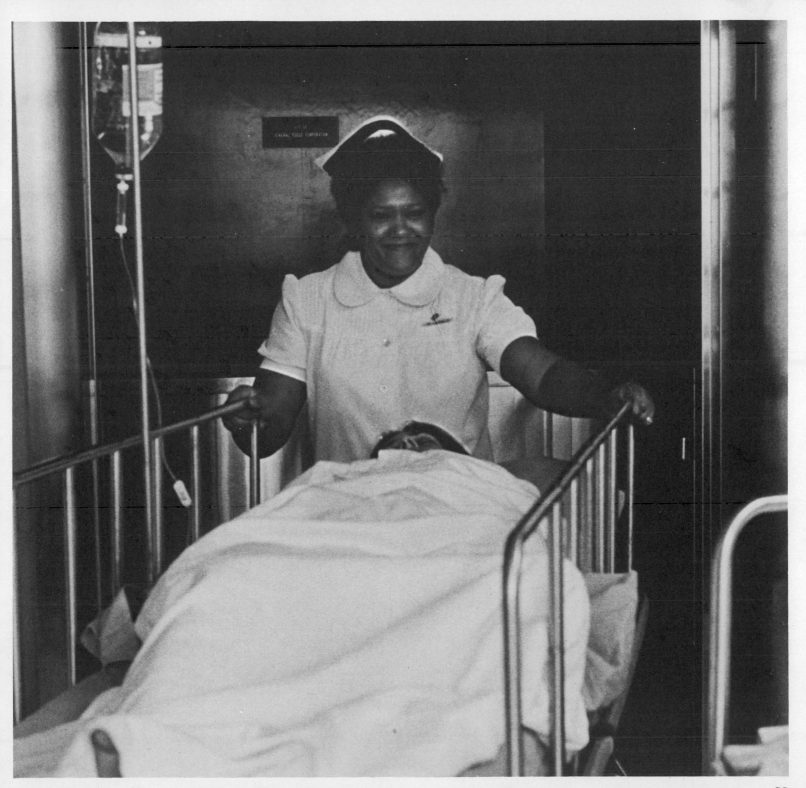

The little thing of no breakfast before an operation can loom large, especially to a child under five years old. It is a child's first hint that what he fears is true: Mommy and Daddy are abandoning him, are taking away their protection just when he needs it most. You can explain why: If a person eats before an operation, the food can make him throw up. You are protecting him from that.

To many children, not being allowed to wear one's own pajamas comes as a shock too. These people are taking away too much—because it is as though his clothes were his very skin, that look like him, that say who he is, and now there is too little left. Your hospital may have different rules, but in this hospital no one will mind a small thing like underpants if they help hold body and soul together.

Jill takes her clothes off and puts hospital clothes on. She still has her own underpants. She wants something to eat, but people aren't allowed to eat before an operation.

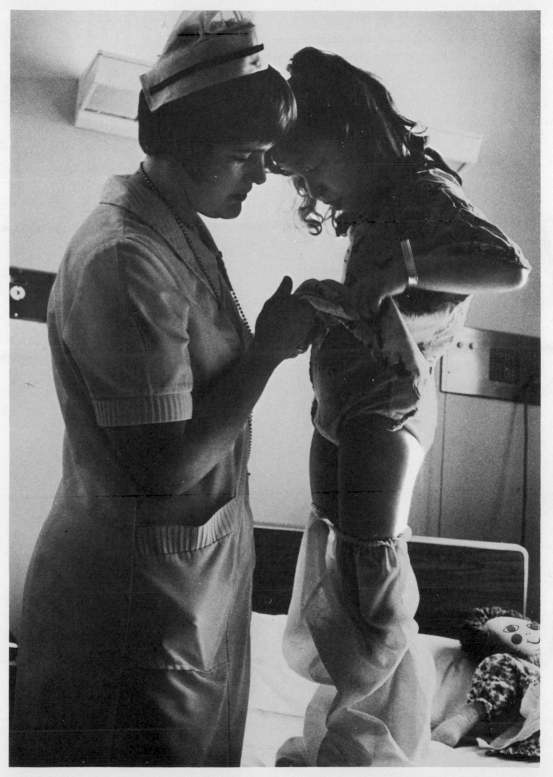

People want your blood, and people want your urine. What, a child wonders, could their motive be? A child might think a blood test was someone coming at him with a weapon to hurt him. Or he might worry that it is dangerous to lose blood from his body. Or he may even wonder if people can find out, by examining his blood, bad things he has thought or done.

The simplest explanation to give a child is: The doctor needs to know how strong and healthy you are inside and outside. He can see the outside of you, and he can see into your ears and nose and mouth. But blood and urine come from way inside your body, so that is how he checks you there.

And now, it's time to get a blood test. It will hurt, but it won't keep on hurting.

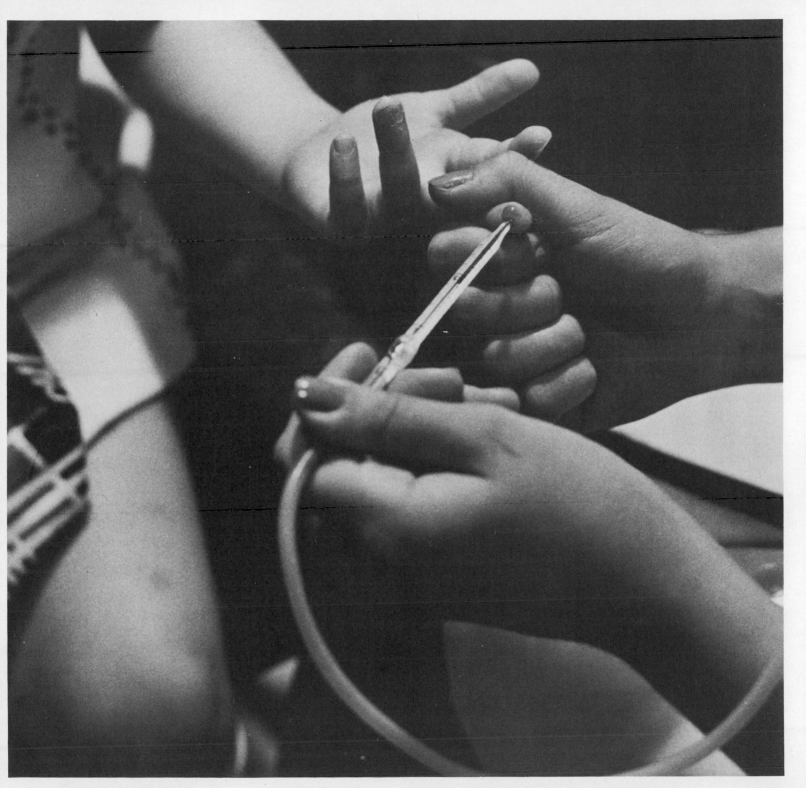

Explanations will help. But so will plain old sympathy. We are sorry; we can say so. We know how it feels, because things happened to us once, when we were little. Jill's father remembers when he had appendicitis: He wanted to stay lying on the couch at home, even though he hurt so much, just so he wouldn't have to go to the hospital. Jill's mother remembers when a surgeon made stitches in her arm —see the scar? And when her own tonsils were taken out. They can both say the things they felt then. They can understand how Jill feels now; Jill can see that they came through all right.

When the doctors and the nurses hear parents talking so seriously with their child, it helps them too. Maybe they don't have to be so make-believe cheery—here are people who can talk plainly to one another about how they really feel.

A new doctor comes to check Jill's ears and throat. She is kind, but it is hard for Jill. There are so many strangers in a hospital.

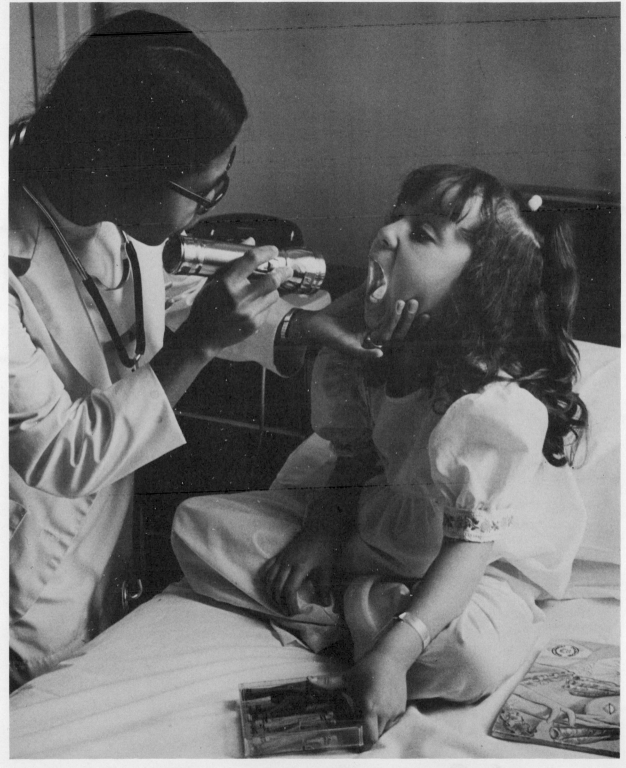

A child's own mommy and daddy have always known and loved and cared for his body. Now strangers are doing things to him and he has nothing to say about it. That is why Jill's mother makes sure she can be with her even for a shot, and even though the nurse may think she is in the way. She has always cared for Jill's body; she shows it is still her concern now.

This is what Jill doesn't like: Not having breakfast, not being home, hospital clothes, blood tests, making pee pee in a bottle and shots.

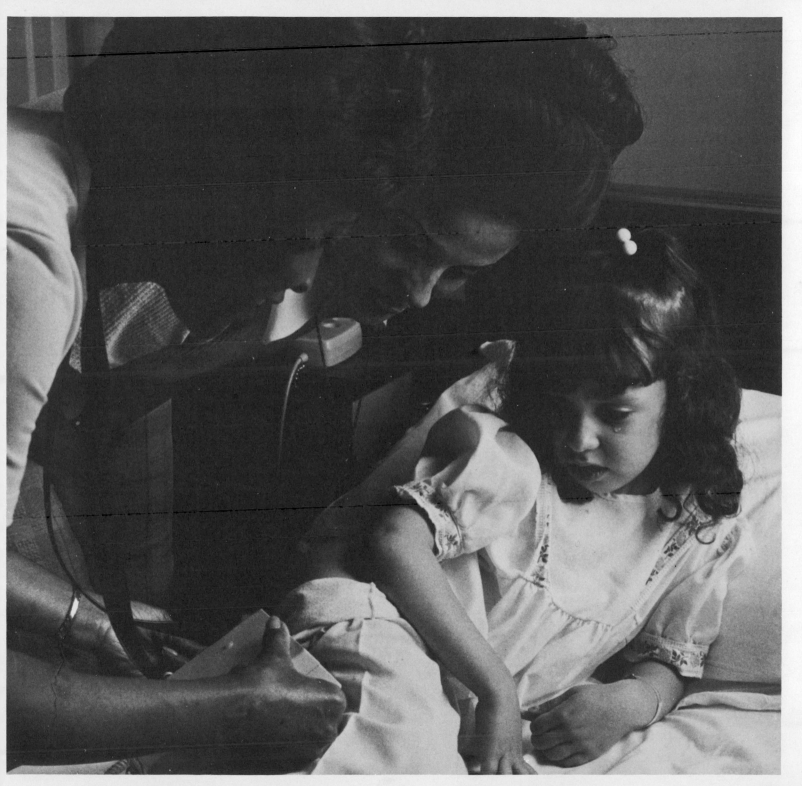

A grownup is concerned about a child's body in a different way than the child himself. A grownup knows more—weighs what is serious, what is not; measures the big risks, discounts the trivial. A grownup can say, "It's just a tonsillectomy. There's nothing to worry about. It will only take a few minutes." But at three, or five, a tonsil is as crucial as a kidney, an hour as long as a day. A knife, if it cuts at all, might cut anywhere. An older child might think if he is unconscious he could do bad things, tell secrets, go wild or never wake up again.

What will help a child sort out confusion is the truth. You said only his tonsils would be cut—sure enough, only his tonsils were cut. You said it would hurt afterwards —sure enough, it hurts. What you tell him comes true. What he fears does not.

Now Jill gets on a bed with wheels that will take her to the operating room. Mommy is not allowed to go with her. She waits in the hospital room for Jill to come back.

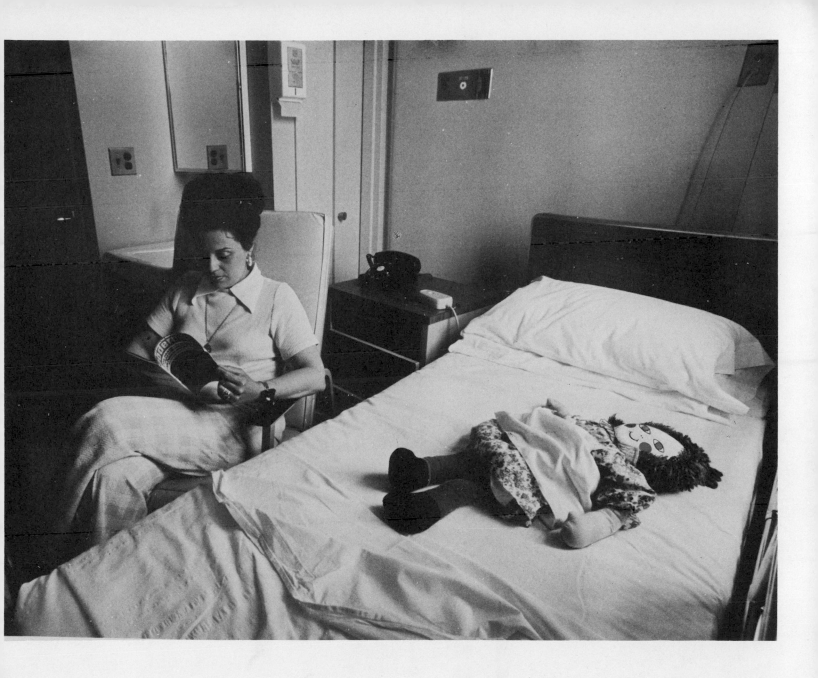

Dodie waits too.

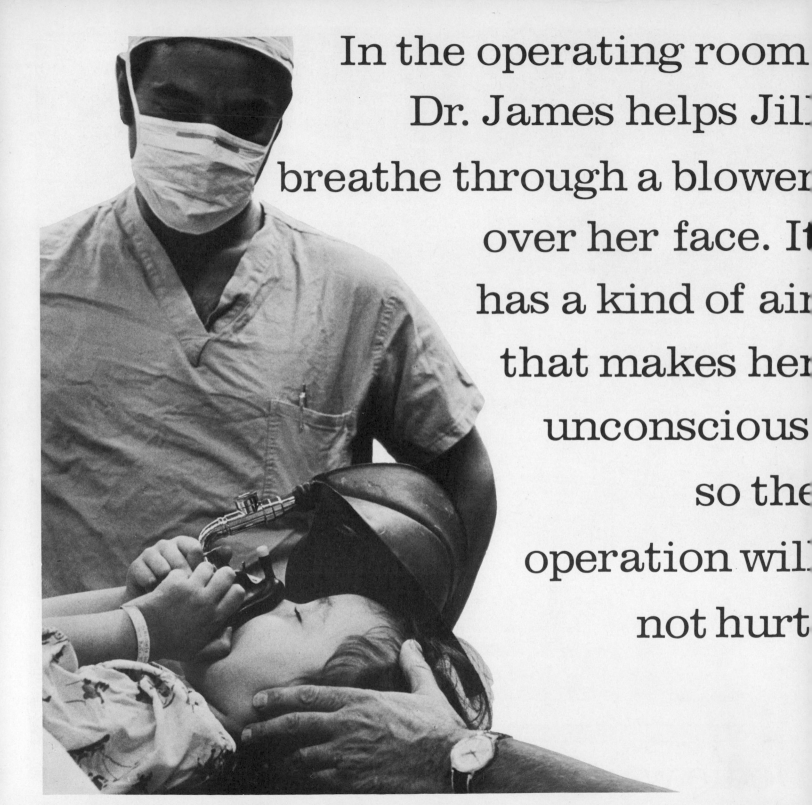

In the operating room
Dr. James helps Jill
breathe through a blower
over her face. It
has a kind of air
that makes her
unconscious
so the
operation will
not hurt

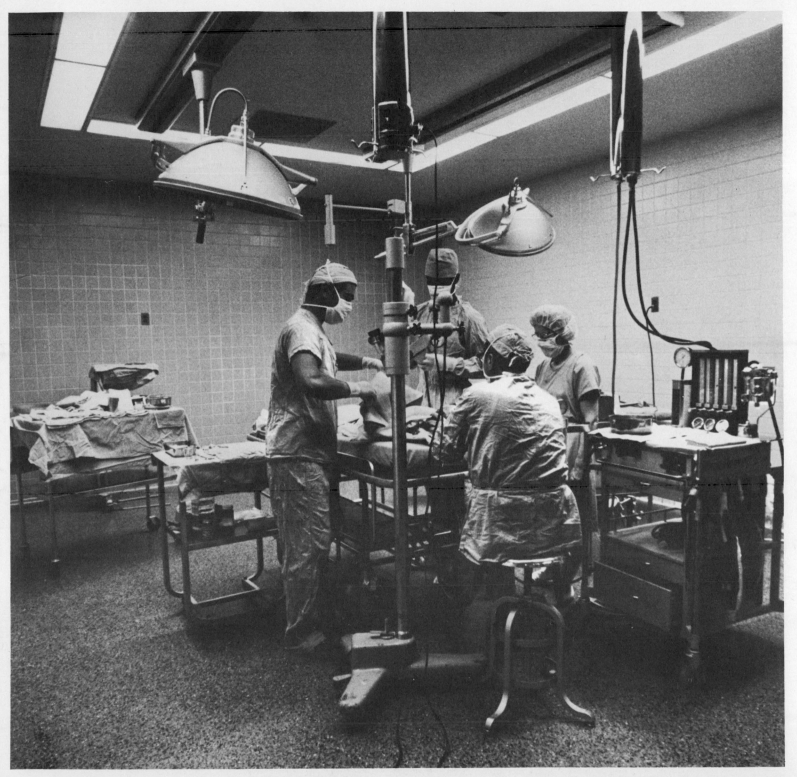

A doctor can help you explain what things in the operating room are, and what they are for.

It is hard to explain anesthesia to a child. It is not "just like going to sleep." It is different—it is called being unconscious.

If people do something that makes you hurt when you are sleeping, you wake up right away. But when you are unconscious people can make noise and do things that would usually hurt—like putting a special instrument in your mouth, way back in your throat, and snipping out your tonsils with it—and you don't feel it, and don't wake up until the doctor has finished. There is another difference too: When you go to sleep at night, you sleep until you aren't tired anymore, and then you wake up and feel good. When you get anesthesia, you don't wake up until the medicine is used up; and when you wake up, you don't feel good at all.

Ask the doctor what kind of anesthesia will be used so you can tell your child what is to come.

When your child is brought back to you, he may not know where he is. He cries. And now his operation hurts. You must be strong and close, comforting him with your calm.

To answer other questions your child has about these pictures, show them to a doctor or nurse and ask what things are, and what they are for.

When the anesthesia wears off, Jill is in the recovery room. She doesn't see her mommy. Now there is a strong pain in her throat. She feels pretty sick. She has no more tonsils. She cries.

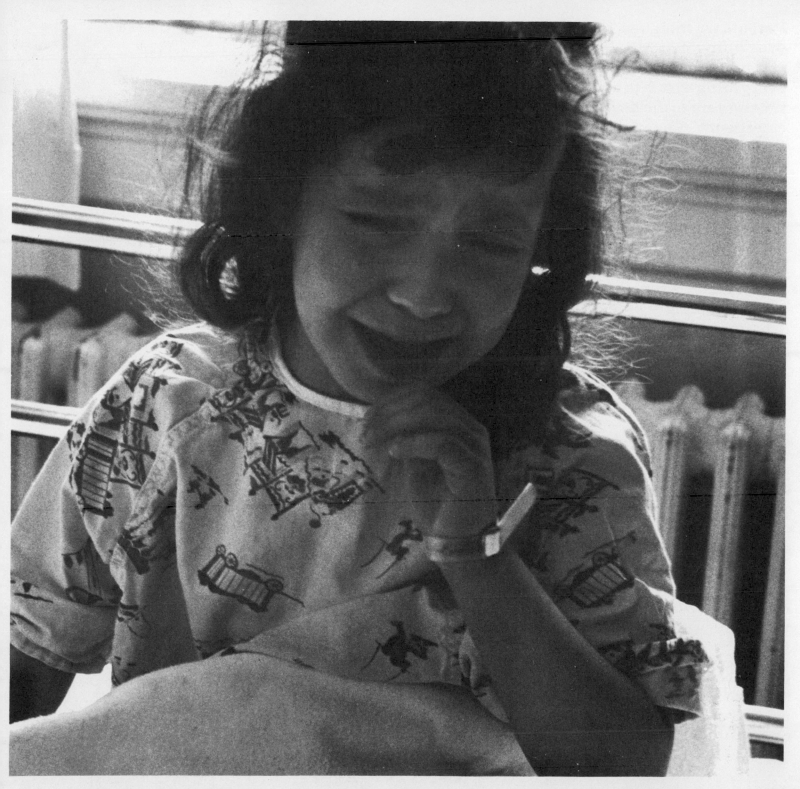

Parents try their best to explain everything that will happen; but still no one can always know everything that is to come. Sometimes going to the hospital is an emergency. Sometimes the unexpected happens and no one could have known. All you can do then is be there. Your child needs you. We know that for sure. We know for sure that the worst thing that happens to a child under 5 or 6 years old in the hospital is that he is separated from his parents. Even older than five, when a child's biggest worries are more what will happen to his body or what anesthesia could do to him, a child is scared without his mommy or daddy around. He feels weaker, because they are his strength. He gives up trying to tell what he feels if they are not there to tell it to. He gets sad, or babyish, or turned off to everything. It doesn't matter whether it is a small cut or a serious injury. He is not big enough yet. You are.

But Mommy didn't go away.

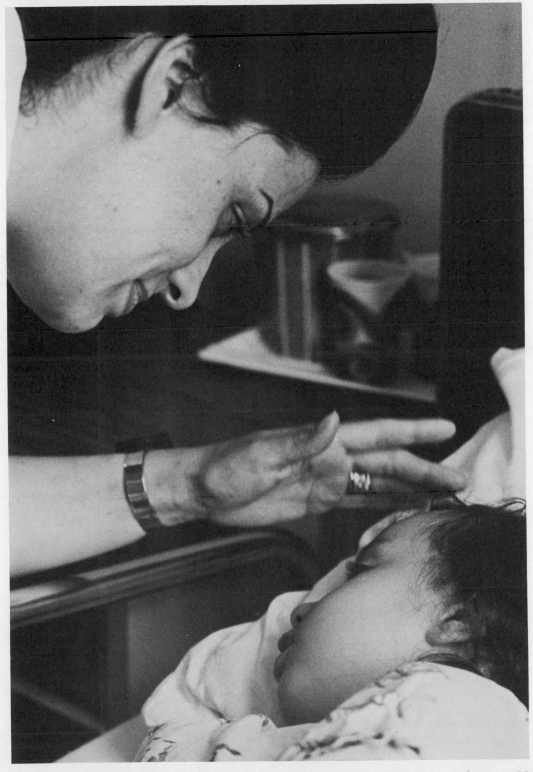

We are only at the beginning of a
time when doctors and nurses and
parents and children can talk to
one another about these problems.
No one is very used to it yet. The
hospital may say, "No parents
overnight." The nurse may tell you
your child behaves better when
you're not there. The doctor may
think you're overprotective. It
may be hard, but you can insist
you will stay for the night, even
just in a chair, absolutely if your
child is under six, possibly up to
eight. When you can't be there you
can make arrangements for your
child to call you on the telephone,
or for the nurse to remind him
where you are and when you will
be back. You can be the one to give
your child a bath or a bedpan, hold
him while he has a shot, go with
him to get an x-ray. Maybe someone won't like it or will make you
feel foolish, but you can insist.
You and your child will both feel
better . . . together.

Jill will stay in the hospital the whole night.

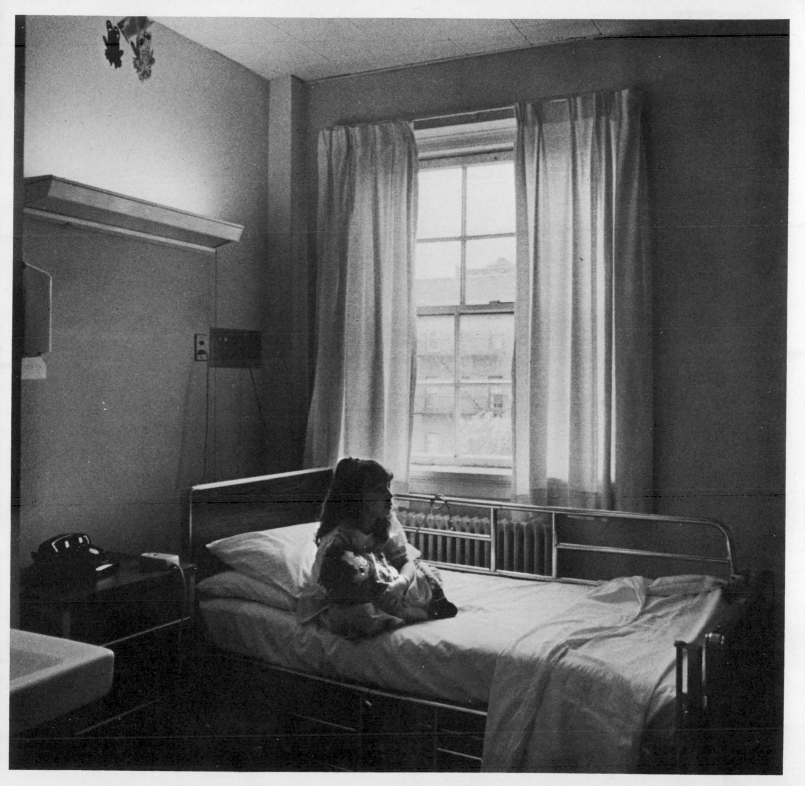

And now Jill does feel better. So do her mother and father. They feel like saying "Hooray! That's over with!" But it isn't. There are other children Jill has seen, ones who can't go home. There are other thoughts Jill has had, ones she has not told. There are experiences she has had that no one knew were important, and conclusions she has drawn that no one guessed. There are things that happened that no one could have predicted or prepared her for. They came as a surprise and made Jill afraid or mad.

Because these things that have happened inside a child are unique to him, only he can tell you about them. And a mother or father can listen to a child like no one else can—can catch the words of a murmured song he has just this moment invented, watch the small events in a game he has just now made up, take seriously some silly thing he says and agree, "A child *could* think that."

In the morning, some of the children can come into the playroom. Jill can go home today.

One little girl played she was a baby robin so mommy robin would have to feed her for a long time after her operation. She felt it was safer to be a baby again. One little boy had tantrums when he couldn't have his own way. He had to be boss so he wouldn't feel helpless the way he had in the hospital. One child might tail after his mother about the house, another might suddenly be scared of bugs or have to wear his boots everywhere or have trouble going to sleep. Each is trying in his own way to get over what has happened to him.

Jill eats and shouts to prove to herself that things are really all right down there in her throat. But she wants a bandaid for every little scratch too, just to be sure.

At home Jill eats potatoes and chicken and red jello. She shouts in a very loud voice. She's fine.

The hard things in life take a long time to get used to. Jill's father goes over again and again the pictures Jill took in the hospital. There are some things he didn't see and Jill can explain them to him. Jill's mother tells her little daughter this hospital story many times. It is her story. It is hard, but it belongs to her life as much as sunshine and hamburgers and Dodie. It too will make her strong.

But sometimes Dodie still needs operations.